Saints

Novena and Prayers

By
Mary Mark Wickenhiser, FSP

BOOKS & MEDIA
Boston

Nihil Obstat: Rev. John E. Sassani

Imprimatur: ✢ Most Rev. Richard G. Lennon
Apostolic Administrator of
the Archdiocese of Boston
March 17, 2003

ISBN 0-8198-7073-0

Cover art: Tom Kinarney

Texts of the New Testament used in this work are taken from *The St. Paul Catholic Edition of the New Testament,* translated by Mark A. Wauck. Copyright © 1992, Society of St. Paul. All rights reserved.

Texts of the Psalms used in this work are translated by Manuel Miguens. Copyright © 1995, Daughters of St. Paul.

All rights reserved. No part of this book may be reproduced or transmitted in any form or by any means, electronic or mechanical, including photocopying, recording or by any information storage and retrieval system, without permission in writing from the publisher.

Copyright © 2003, Daughters of St. Paul

Printed and published in the U.S.A. by Pauline Books & Media, 50 Saint Pauls Avenue, Boston MA 02130-3491.

www.pauline.org

Pauline Books & Media is the publishing house of the Daughters of St. Paul, an international congregation of women religious serving the Church with the communications media.

1 2 3 4 5 6 7 8 9   08 07 06 05 04 03

Contents

What Is a Novena? ---------------------- 5

St. Dymphna --------------------------- 9

Morning Prayer ---------------------- 13

Novena to St. Dymphna ----------- 19

Prayers for Various Needs --------- 23

Evening Prayer ----------------------- 31

What Is a Novena?

The Catholic tradition of praying novenas has its roots in the earliest days of the Church. In the Acts of the Apostles we read that after the ascension of Jesus, the apostles returned to Jerusalem, to the upper room, where "They all devoted themselves single-mindedly to prayer, along with some women and Mary the Mother of Jesus and his brothers" (Acts 1:14). Jesus had instructed his disciples to wait for the coming of the Holy Spirit, and on the day of Pentecost, the Spirit of the Lord came to them. This prayer of the first Christian community was the first "novena." Based on this, Christians have always prayed for various needs, trusting that God both hears and answers prayer.

The word "novena" is derived from the Latin term *novem*, meaning nine. In biblical times numbers held deep symbolism for people. The number "three," for example, symbolized perfection, fullness, completeness. The number nine—three times three—symbolized perfection times perfection. Novenas developed because it was thought that—symbolically speaking—nine days represented the perfect amount of time to pray. The ancient Greeks and Romans had the custom of mourning for nine days after a death. The early Christian Church offered Mass for the deceased for nine consecutive days. During the Middle Ages novenas in preparation for solemn feasts became popular, as did novenas to particular saints.

Whether a novena is made solemnly—in a parish church in preparation for a feastday—or in the privacy of one's home, as Christians we never really pray alone. Through the waters of Baptism we have become members of the body of Christ and are thereby united to every other member of Christ's Mystical Body. When we pray, we are spiritually united with all the other members.

Just as we pray for each other while here on earth, those who have gone before us and are united with God in heaven can pray for us and intercede for us as well. We Catholics use the term "communion of saints" to refer to this exchange of spiritual help among the members of the Church on earth, those who have died and are being purified, and the saints in heaven.

While nothing can replace the celebration of Mass and the sacraments as the Church's highest form of prayer, devotions have a special place in Catholic life. Devotions such as the Stations of the Cross can help us enter into the sufferings of Jesus and give us an understanding of his personal love for us. The mysteries of the rosary can draw us into meditating on the lives of Jesus and Mary. Devotions to the saints can help us witness to our faith and encourage us in our commitment to lead lives of holiness and service as they did.

How to use this booklet

The morning and evening prayers are modeled on the Liturgy of the Hours, following its pattern of psalms, scripture readings and intercessions.

We suggest that during the novena you make time in your schedule to pray the morning prayer and evening prayer. If you are able, try to also set aside a time during the day when you can pray the novena and any other particular prayer(s) you have chosen. Or you can recite the devotional prayers at the conclusion of the morning or evening prayer. What is important is to pray with expectant faith and confidence in a loving God who will answer our prayers in the way that will most benefit us. The Lord "satisfies the thirsty, and the hungry he fills with good things" (Ps 107:9).

St. Dymphna

Patroness of Those Who Suffer with Mental or Emotional Problems

Sometimes called the "Lily of Eire," St. Dymphna has gained great popularity as the patroness of those who suffer with mental or emotional problems. Historically, little can be verified about the details of her life. But ancient traditions give us the following account.

St. Dymphna was born in Ireland sometime in the early 600s. Her father, a petty king of Oriel, was not Christian, but her mother was a devout Catholic. At an early age Dymphna was placed under the care of a devout Christian woman who prepared her for baptism. Father Gerebran, a chaplain for the Catholics in the household, gave Dymphna religious instructions and taught her how to read.

When Dymphna was a teenager her mother died. Her father wanted to remarry, and he desired to find a woman who would be like his first wife in beauty and character. Whether it was brought on by grief or another cause, the king slipped into some form of mental illness. In this state he began to desire to marry Dymphna, for her beauty and grace constantly reminded him of his deceased wife.

Shocked at the proposal, Dymphna consulted Father Gerebran, who advised her to flee the country immediately. Dymphna set out for the continent, accompanied by the priest and two servants. They landed on the coast near Antwerp and traveled to a village named Gheel.

When the king discovered that Dymphna had escaped, he searched for her and eventually traced her to Gheel. At first Dymphna's father tried to persuade her to return with him, but Father Gerebran opposed him. The king ordered that the priest be put to death, and the king's men struck the priest with their swords.

Dymphna resisted her father's attempts to induce her to return with him. In a fit of rage, the father drew a dagger from his belt and struck her a mortal blow. She was only about fifteen years old. Tradition puts the date of her death as May 15, which was assigned as her feastday on the old liturgical calendar. The year was probably between 620 and 640.

The records of Dymphna's life and death state that the bodies of the two martyred saints (Dymphna and Father Gerebran) lay on the ground for a long time before the inhabitants of Gheel brought them to a cave for burial. But after several years, the villagers decided to give the bodies a more suitable burial. When workmen removed the heap of black earth at the cave's entrance, they were astonished to find two beautiful tombs, whiter than snow, which were carved from stone as if by an angel's hands. When Dymphna's coffin was opened, they found in it a red tile bearing the inscription: "Here lies the holy virgin and martyr, Dymphna." The remains of the saints were placed in a small church. Later, a much larger church of St. Dymphna was built on the site where the bodies were first buried.

As people paid homage to the saints, miraculous cures began to occur. Gradually, St. Dymphna's fame as patroness of those who suffer with mental and emotional problems spread widely, and many such persons came to the shrine on pilgrimages. Remarkable cures helped spread devotion to Dymphna. At first, mentally ill patients were lodged in a small annex built onto the church. Then the families living in Gheel began to take them into their homes.

From this beginning Gheel developed into a town famous for its care of the mentally ill. An institution called the "Infirmary of St. Elizabeth," conducted by the Sisters of St. Augustine, was later built for the hospital care of the patients. After some time spent in the institution, most patients are placed in a home of one of the families of Gheel.

In May 1939 a chapel was dedicated to St. Dymphna on the grounds of the Massillon State Hospital, Massillon, Ohio. The *League of St. Dymphna*, offering many spiritual benefits for both living and deceased, has also been established there. Further information about this League may be obtained from:

National Shrine of St. Dymphna
3000 Erie St., P.O. Box 4
Massillon, OH 44648-0004

Marianne Lorraine Trouvé, FSP

Morning Prayer

Morning prayer is a time to give praise and thanks to God, to remind ourselves that he is the source of all beauty and goodness. Lifting one's heart and mind to God in the early hours of the day puts one's life into perspective: God is our loving Creator who watches over us with tenderness and is always ready to embrace us with his compassion and mercy.

While at prayer, try to create a prayerful atmosphere, perhaps with a burning candle to remind you that Christ is the light who illumines your daily path, an open Bible to remind you that the Lord is always present, a crucifix to remind you of the depths of God's love for you. Soft music can also contribute to a serene and prayerful mood.

If a quiet place is not available, or if you pray as you commute to and from work, remember that the God who loves you is present everywhere and hears your prayer no matter the setting.

It is good to give thanks and praise the Lord our God,
to proclaim his love in the morning.
Glory to the Father, and to the Son, and to the Holy Spirit,
as it was in the beginning, is now, and will be forever. Amen.

Psalm 34

*Lord, you are close to the brokenhearted;
you save the troubled in spirit.*

I will bless the LORD at all times;
his praise is ever on my lips.
It is in the LORD that my soul shall boast.
The humble shall hear of it and rejoice.
Join me in celebrating the greatness of the LORD,
and let us extol his name together.

I sought the LORD and he answered me;
he delivered me from all my fears.
Those who gazed on him were radiant with joy
and their faces were not made to blush.
The afflicted ones cried out and the LORD heard,
and saved them from all their troubles.

Taste and see how good the LORD is.
Happy the person who takes refuge in him.

Glory to the Father....

Psalm 18

*Lord, you brighten my darkness;
your promises are true.*

The LORD is my stronghold, my fortress,
   my rescuer,
my God is my rock where I take refuge.
He is my shield, my saving power, my mainstay.
I call on the LORD, worthy of all praise,
and I am saved from my enemies.

In my distress, I called to the LORD and
from his temple my God heard my voice;
my cry came to his presence, to his very ears.
This is why I will praise you, LORD,
   among the nations,
and sing psalms to your name.

Glory to the Father...

The Word of God
Matthew 6:25–26

Yesterday has already slipped from our grasp. Tomorrow is beyond our reach. Today is the day we are given to focus our energies on the here and now—to be aware of God acting in the present moment.

Do not worry about life, what you will eat, or about your body, what you will wear; is not life more than food, and the body more than clothing? Look at the birds of the sky—they neither sow nor reap nor gather into barns, yet your Heavenly Father feeds them; are you not worth more than they are?

Today is the day the Lord has made; I will rejoice and be glad.

From prayer one draws the strength needed to meet the challenges of daily life as a committed follower of Jesus Christ, and as such to be a living sign of the Lord's loving presence in the world.

Intercessions

*G*racious God, I thank and praise you for the gift of this new day. With confidence I come into your presence to place my petitions before you and pray:

Response: *May your grace be with me, Lord.*

Grant that I may recognize your loving Providence at work in the events of this day. **R.**

Grant that I seek to see your face in everyone I meet today. **R.**

Grant that I may be a source of joy and consolation for the brokenhearted. **R.**

Grant that in all I say and do today I may be a living witness of your love and mercy **R.**

Grant that all those I love may be kept from harm this day. **R.**

(Add your own general intentions and your particular intentions for this novena.)

Conclude your intercession by praying to our Heavenly Father in the words Jesus taught us:

Our Father, who art in heaven, hallowed be thy name; thy kingdom come; thy will be done on earth as it is in heaven. Give us this day our daily bread, and forgive us our trespasses, as we forgive those who trespass against us, and lead us not into temptation, but deliver us from evil. Amen.

Closing Prayer

*L*ord, our God, source of all goodness, guide me according to your will. Grant that I may spend this day in joy of spirit and peace of mind, faithful to your teaching and free from all sin. I ask this in the name of Jesus Christ, your Son. Amen.

Let us praise the Lord

And give him thanks.

Novena to St. Dymphna

St. Dymphna, virgin and martyr of purity,
—intercede for us to God.
You were a loving disciple of Jesus and a compassionate servant of those in need,
—present my prayer of praise and supplication to God.

God of goodness and mercy, I praise and thank you for the many blessings I have received through you generous love. As I honor your servant, St. Dymphna, for the love of purity you granted her, I ask for the grace to remain steadfast in my love for you so that I may spend my life doing good and avoiding all that is not in accord with your will for me.

Trusting in your goodness, and with confidence in your power to heal, I humbly ask, through the intercession of St. Dymphna, for this grace: *(mention your specific intention)*. May all nations come to know the power of your love and the unfailing gift of your mercy, so that one day we may all glorify you with all the saints in heaven. Amen.

Our Father, who art in heaven, hallowed be thy name; thy kingdom come; thy will be done on earth as it is in heaven. Give us this day our daily bread, and forgive us our trespasses, as we forgive those who trespass against us, and lead us not into temptation, but deliver us from evil. Amen.

Hail Mary, full of grace, the Lord is with you. Blessed are you among women, and blessed is the fruit of your womb,

Jesus. Holy Mary, Mother of God, pray for us sinners, now and at the hour of our death. Amen.

Glory to the Father, and to the Son, and to the Holy Spirit, as it was in the beginning, is now, and will be forever. Amen.

St. Dymphna, virgin and martyr, hear my prayers and answer my petition.

O God, we ask you through the intercession of your servant, St. Dymphna, who sealed with her blood the love she had for you, to grant relief to those in our midst who suffer from mental illness and/or psychological disorders. Through Christ, your Son, our Lord. Amen.

Prayers for Various Needs

Prayer in Time of Distress

St. Dymphna, compassionate and faithful friend to all who rely on your intercession, you are a source of consolation and support in time of distress. In my need I come to you to seek your help *(mention your request)*. The cross that I carry seems too heavy for me to bear; I feel discouraged and helpless in the face of my brokenness. Intercede for me that I may once again know the power of the Lord's redeeming love and the shield of his comfort in my life. Teach me, gentle patron, how to live by faith in Jesus' promise that he is with me always. Teach me how to live in hope, relying on the Lord's saving power to bring me through this time of pain and suffering. Teach me how to live in love that I may be a light in the darkness for others.

Glory to the Father….

Prayer for Acceptance and Trust

Lord our God, you led the holy virgin and martyr St. Dymphna through danger and trial and gave her a glorious crown in heaven. Through her intercession grant that I, too, may trust in your abiding presence in my time of suffering and trial. Give me the strength I need to face my situation with courage and hope. Help me to unite my sufferings to those of Jesus, so that I may follow your Son more closely and rejoice forever with him in heaven. I ask this through Jesus Christ, our Lord. Amen.

Prayer for Someone Suffering from Depression

Almighty and eternal God, healer of those who trust in you, through the intercession of St. Dymphna, hear my prayer for *(name)*. In your tender mercy, lift the burden of depression from her/him and restore her/him to full emotional health that she/he may give you thanks, praise your name, and proclaim your wondrous love to all. I ask this through Christ your Son, our Lord. Amen.

Our Father, Hail Mary, Glory to the Father….

Prayer for Healing

Compassionate St. Dymphna, through the power of your heavenly Spouse, Jesus Christ, you obtained health of mind and body for all who called upon you in their need. With a humble, trustful heart, and with faith in the Lord's healing power, I ask, through your intercession, to be restored to mental health and/or emotional well-being. Confident in the Lord's promise that whatever we ask in his name will be granted, I praise God for the many blessings I have already received from his generous love, and look to the day when I can glorify him with you and all the saints in heaven. Amen.

Our Father, Hail Mary, Glory to the Father….

St. Dymphna, pray for me.

Prayer for Those Suffering from Mental or Emotional Disorders

Lord Jesus Christ, you have willed that St. Dymphna should be invoked by her devotees as patroness of those who suffer from mental or emotional disorders. You have also willed that her protective interest in these persons should inspire all believers and be an ideal of charity for caregivers. Grant that, through the prayers of this youthful martyr, all those who suffer from mental illness and/or psychological disorders may be helped and consoled. In particular, I recommend to you... *(mention those you wish to pray for)*.

Divine Healer, be pleased to hear the prayers of St. Dymphna and of your Blessed Mother, health of the sick and comforter of the afflicted, on behalf of those whom I recommend to the love and compassion of your Sacred Heart. Give them the consolation they need and, if it be your will, the healing they so much desire. May we all serve your suffering members with selfless love until the day we are united forever in heaven with you, who lives and reigns with the Father, in the unity of the Holy Spirit, forever and ever. Amen.

Prayer of Praise and Thanksgiving

It is fitting for us to praise and thank God for the graces and privileges he has bestowed upon the saints. Devotees of St. Dymphna may pray the following act of thanksgiving during their novena.

Lord Jesus, I praise, glorify, and bless you for all the graces and privileges you have bestowed upon your servant, the virgin and martyr, St. Dymphna. By her merits grant me your grace, and through her intercession help me in all my needs. At the hour of my death be with me until that time when I can join the saints in heaven to praise you forever and ever. Amen.

Litany in Honor of St. Dymphna

(For private use)

Lord, have mercy on us.
Christ, have mercy on us.
Lord, have mercy on us.
Christ, hear us.
Christ, graciously hear us.

God the Father of heaven, *have mercy on us.*
God the Son, Redeemer of the world,
    have mercy on us.
God the Holy Spirit, *have mercy on us.*
Holy Trinity, one God, *have mercy on us.*

Holy Mary, Virgin and Mother of God, *pray for us.*
Health of the sick, *pray for us.*

Comforter of the afflicted, *pray for us.*
Help of Christians, *pray for us.*
St. Dymphna, virgin and martyr, *pray for us.*
St. Dymphna, beautiful in soul and body,
    pray for us.
St. Dymphna, docile to the example set by your
    devout mother, *pray for us.*
St. Dymphna, obedient to your holy confessor,
    pray for us.
St. Dymphna, who fled the court of your father to
    escape immorality, *pray for us.*
St. Dymphna, who chose a life of poverty on earth,
    to store up treasures in heaven, *pray for us.*
St. Dymphna, who sought strength and consola-
    tion in prayer, *pray for us.*
St. Dymphna, faithful spouse of the divine Bride-
    groom, *pray for us.*
St. Dymphna, devoted to the Mother of God,
    pray for us.
St. Dymphna, martyr of holy purity, *pray for us.*
St. Dymphna, shining example of Christian youth,
    pray for us.
St. Dymphna, renowned for many miracles,
    pray for us.
St. Dymphna, glory of Ireland and Belgium,
    pray for us.
St. Dymphna, compassionate toward those in
    need, *pray for us.*

St. Dymphna, protector against mental illness and emotional disorders, *pray for us.*
St. Dymphna, consoler of the afflicted, *pray for us.*
St. Dymphna, friend of the helpless, *pray for us.*
St. Dymphna, hope for those who are depressed, *pray for us.*
St. Dymphna, light of those in mental darkness, *pray for us.*
St. Dymphna, patroness of those who suffer from mental illness or emotional disorders, *pray for us.*

That we may love the Lord our God with all our hearts and above all things, *we beseech you, hear us.*
That we may hate sin and avoid all occasions of sin, *we beseech you, hear us.*
That we may safeguard the virtue of purity in heart and body, *we beseech you, hear us.*
That we may receive the sacraments frequently, *we beseech you, hear us.*
That we may be granted the spirit of prayer, *we beseech you, hear us.*
That we may be humble and obedient, seeking God's will in our lives, *we beseech you, hear us.*
That we may seek to have confidence in God during times of suffering, *we beseech you, hear us.*

That we may persevere in God's love until the end of our lives, *we beseech you, hear us.*
In times of sickness, disease, war, and persecution, *we beseech you, hear us.*
In our last illness, *we beseech you, hear us.*
At the hour of death, *we beseech you, hear us.*

Lamb of God, you take away the sins of the world, *spare us, O Lord.*
Lamb of God, you take away the sins of the world, *graciously hear us, O Lord.*
Lamb of God, you take away the sins of the world, *have mercy on us.*

V. Pray for us, St. Dymphna,
R. That we may become worthy of the promises of Christ.

Let us pray.

O God, you gave St. Dymphna to your Church as an example of virtue, and willed that she should seal her faith with her innocent blood. Grant that we who honor her as patroness of those afflicted with mental illness or psychological disorders, may continue to enjoy her powerful intercession and protection and attain eternal life. Through Christ our Lord. Amen.

—Taken from common sources

Evening Prayer

As this day draws to a close we place ourselves in an attitude of thanksgiving. We take time to express our gratitude to a loving God for his abiding presence. We thank him for the gift of the day and all it brought with it. We thank him for all the things we were able to achieve throughout the day, and we entrust to him the concerns we have for tomorrow.

Let my prayer come before you, O God,
like fragrant incense upon your altar.
Glory to the Father, and to the Son, and to the
    Holy Spirit,
as it was in the beginning, is now, and will be
    forever. Amen.

Take a few moments for a brief examination of conscience. Reflect on the ways God acted in your life today, how you responded to his invitations to think, speak, and act in a more Christ-like manner, and in what ways you would like to be a more faithful disciple tomorrow.

For the times I acted or spoke unkindly toward others:
Jesus, Son of David, have mercy on me.
For the times I was untruthful or unforgiving:
Jesus, Son of David, have mercy on me.
For the times I acted out of anger, jealousy, or self-interest:
Jesus, Son of David, have mercy on me.
For the times I engaged in hurtful gossip:
Jesus, Son of David, have mercy on me.
For the times… (any other petitions for pardon).
   (Or any other Act of Sorrow)

Psalm 84

Lord, happy are they who find their strength in you.

How lovely, O LORD, is your dwelling place.
My soul yearns, yes, longs for the courts of the LORD.
My heart and my flesh joyfully shout for the living God.
By your altars, O LORD, my king and my God,
the sparrow also finds a home
and the swallow her nest where she lays her young.

Happy those who abide in your house!
They continue to sing your praises.
Happy are they whose strength is in you.
One day in your courts is better than a thousand
 elsewhere.
To stand at the threshold of God's house is better
than to live in the dwellings of wickedness.
Truly, you, Lord God, are a sun and shield;
You, Lord grant favor and splendor;
you will not withhold any good from those who
 live an upright life.
O Lord, happy those who trust in you.

The Word of God
John 15:4–5, 7

Our daily activities take on their true meaning when Christ abides at the center of our lives. When we abide in the love he offers us, we experience an interior peace that gives reassurance during the difficult times and increases the joy of the good times.

I am the vine, you are the branches.
Whoever abides in me, and I them,
 will bear much fruit,
For apart from me you can do nothing.
If you abide in me, and my works abide in you,

ask whatever you wish and it will happen for you.

I hope in you, Lord, I trust in your word.

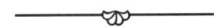

In prayer we bring before the Lord our own needs and the needs of those we love. We take time to consider the needs of the world and intercede for those who do not or cannot pray. We offer petitions for the improvement of the human condition so that our world will be a better place to live, and all people may contribute to building up God's kingdom here on earth.

Intercessions

God of compassion and love, we thank you for the gifts you have given us this day. With confidence in your loving care, we offer our needs and the needs of all humanity.

Response: *Lord, hear our prayer, through the intercession of St. Dymphna.*

That those who minister in your name may lead lives of holiness and seek to be true witnesses to the Gospel message of love and compassion, we pray. **R.**

That world leaders may govern with integrity and seek to protect the rights of all human persons especially the underprivileged and the disabled, we pray. **R.**

That all those who suffer in body, mind, or spirit (*especially N.*), may know the healing touch of the Divine Master, we pray. **R.**

That those living in treatment facilities because they are unable to care for themselves may experience the patience and compassion of loving caregivers, we pray. **R.**

That those who bear the hardship of mental illness and have no one to care for them may know the comfort of a loving God and the kindness and support of the human family, we pray. **R.**

That those who are anxious or depressed because they are without a job and a home may have the strength of spirit to seek professional assistance, we pray. **R.**

That those dedicated to medical research in the field of mental and emotional health may know the joy that comes from helping others, we pray. **R.**

That all who have died, especially those who have suffered an untimely death as a result of mental illness or emotional ill-health, may soon enjoy light, happiness, and peace in the joy of eternal life, we pray. **R.**

(Add any other spontaneous intentions and your particular intentions for this novena.)

Conclude your intercessions by praying to our Heavenly Father in the words Jesus taught us:

Our Father....

Closing Prayer

Good and gracious Lord, receive our evening prayer. Guard us from evil and grant us a restful sleep, so that with the coming of a new day we may serve you with renewed strength and joy. We ask this in the name of Jesus, your Son. Amen.

Mary, Jesus' Mother and ours, is always ready to intercede for those who ask her help.

Remember, O most gracious Virgin Mary,
that never was it known
that anyone who fled to your protection,
implored your help,
or sought your intercession
was left unaided.
Inspired with this confidence
I fly unto you, O Virgin of Virgins, my Mother.

To you I come, before you I stand,
sinful and sorrowful.
O Mother of the Word Incarnate,
despise not my petitions,
but in your mercy hear and answer me. Amen.

BOOKS & MEDIA

The Daughters of St. Paul operate book and media centers at the following addresses. Visit, call or write the one nearest you today, or find us on the World Wide Web, www.pauline.org

CALIFORNIA
3908 Sepulveda Blvd, Culver City, CA 90230 310-397-8676
5945 Balboa Avenue, San Diego, CA 92111 858-565-9181
46 Geary Street, San Francisco, CA 94108 415-781-5180

FLORIDA
145 S.W. 107th Avenue, Miami, FL 33174 305-559-6715

HAWAII
1143 Bishop Street, Honolulu, HI 96813 808-521-2731
Neighbor Islands call: 800-259-8463

ILLINOIS
172 North Michigan Avenue, Chicago, IL 60601 312-346-4228

LOUISIANA
4403 Veterans Memorial Blvd, Metairie, LA 70006 504-887-7631

MASSACHUSETTS
Rte. 1, 885 Providence Hwy, Dedham, MA 02026 781-326-5385

MISSOURI
9804 Watson Road, St. Louis, MO 63126 314-965-3512

NEW JERSEY
561 U.S. Route 1, Wick Plaza, Edison, NJ 08817 732-572-1200

NEW YORK
150 East 52nd Street, New York, NY 10022 212-754-1110
78 Fort Place, Staten Island, NY 10301 718-447-5071

PENNSYLVANIA
9171-A Roosevelt Blvd, Philadelphia, PA 19114 215-676-9494

SOUTH CAROLINA
243 King Street, Charleston, SC 29401 843-577-0175

TENNESSEE
4811 Poplar Avenue, Memphis, TN 38117 901-761-2987

TEXAS
114 Main Plaza, San Antonio, TX 78205 210-224-8101

VIRGINIA
1025 King Street, Alexandria, VA 22314 703-549-3806

CANADA
3022 Dufferin Street, Toronto, Ontario, Canada M6B 3T5 416-781-9131
1155 Yonge Street, Toronto, Ontario, Canada M4T 1W2 416-934-3440

¡También somos su fuente para libros, videos y música en español!